WHY LIKE EAGLES

by

Frank & Sharon White

All Rights Reserved

Copyright © 2000

This book may not be reproduced for mass distribution or resale without the written permission of the author. Short excerpts may be reprinted for Christian teaching and instruction. To contact the author, email mapleleaf4906@gmail.com

Table of Contents

ACKNOWLEDGEMENTS 1

INTRODUCTION 2

WHY WE WROTE THIS BOOK 4

CHAPTER 1 5
   LOOKING BACK.. 5
   MEET REVEREND TILFORD... 9
   WHAT IS THIS PROCESS? 12
   FRANK'S STORY 14
   A MINISTRY IS BORN.. 16

CHAPTER 2 17
   GOING BACK FOR MORE HEALING 17
   CAN CHRISTIANS HAVE DEMONS? 17
   DELIVERANCE IS MINE... 18
   WHEN GOD HEALS YOU OF YOUR PAST IT MAKES A CHANGE IN YOUR PRESENT................................ 20
   WHO CAN I PRACTICE ON? 21
   OPEN FOR BUSINESS... 24
   THERE'S ALWAYS ROOM TO GROW 26

CHAPTER 3 30
   MINISTERING AT WORK 30
   CAN INTELLECTUALS BE HEALED? 31
   MEETING DR. ED SMITH 36

CHAPTER 4 40

    HEALING FOR MY FAMILY 40
    PRAISE THE LORD FOR MIRACLES! 42

CHAPTER 5 49
    HEALING FOR MY CHURCH FAMILY 49
    JESUS HEALS THEM ALL 51
    LESSONS LEARNED 53

CONCLUSION 54

A PRACTICAL APPLICATION 55
    CASE STUDY A: FEAR 55
    CASE STUDY B: PORNOGRAPHY 57
    CASE STUDY C: ABANDONMENT 59
    CASE STUDY D: MOLESTATION 61
    CASE STUDY E: DIVORCE 62
    CASE STUDY F: ANGER 65

ACKNOWLEDGEMENTS

To my husband, Frank White, you are my co-author and ministry-partner. Thank you for being understanding and supportive of the hours that I spend away from you. I thank God for you every day!

To our children, Vickie, Willie, and Dorthy, for believing your parents could write a book.

To Dr. Alice Hicks, thank you for encouraging me to republish the book. You have been Godsend.

To my friends Barb Neal, and Dr. Alice Hicks, I would like to thank you for your encouragement and believing that I could begin and be successful in this healing ministry. Thank you for your faithfulness as intercessors. I could always call on you and you were always there in prayer.

To Dwaine and Cindy Tilford, God has graced you with a ministry that has borne so much fruit. We thank you for your obedience and your love.

To our church families, thank you for pouring into our lives continually.

INTRODUCTION

This is the story of the journey that my husband Frank and I traveled to receive inner healing and renewal of the mind. During our journeys, God graced us with a healing ministry. This healing ministry is also known as a deliverance ministry in some circles. We use the Transformation Process for genuine recovery and renewing the mind.

What does Transformation mean?

"You were taught, with regard to your former way of life, to put off your old self, which is being corrupted by its deceitful desires; to be made new in the attitude of your minds; and to put on the new self, created to be like God in true righteousness and holiness." Ephesians 4:22-24

The process was given to Dr. Ed Smith, a minister and clinical psychologist. Dr. Smith's concept of the work of God was "I had God in a box." God opened his eyes and gave him a method of healing that lay-people like us could use to help ourselves and others be released from "lies in our past." The lies of the past are those things that keep us from "soaring like eagles" in our present.

At the time of the second publication of this book, we have seen over 1000 people and led them through the inner healing. These individuals have spent between one hour and twenty hours in the healing process. This healing method has proven to have over a 95%

success rate for us. That is literally unheard of in many prayer ministries.

Often, a person experiences healing for a short time and later resumes his or her old way of living. We have not seen this type of short-term healing using the Transformation method. Once Jesus heals you, you will never be in bondage to that memory again.

You can be "free at last!" God can work a miracle in you and make you free of the things that are holding you back. Please read the rest of this book with an open mind and you will learn to "soar like eagles". God Bless You!

- Willie Frank & Sharon White

WHY WE WROTE THIS BOOK

All my life I have had a fear. I was afraid of writing. I chose my career so that I would not have to write. I opted to major in mathematics and go on through an MBA program that would not require a written thesis.

Through inner healing that I experienced using the Transformation method, God taught me that He was the author of the book and I was just His vessel. I was healed of the lie that I "could not write."

This is one of many victories I have won, as God has healed me of many things. This book is written in an amusing fashion yet when things were actually happening in our lives, they were traumatic and painful.

Richard Strauss says it so plainly in his book, **Growing More Like Jesus,** "(Jesus) isn't trying to make us successful businesspeople so we can impress the world with our money and affluence. He isn't trying to make us successful churchmen, so we can amaze people with our organizational and administrative skills. He isn't trying to make us great orators, so we can overwhelm audiences with our persuasive words. He wants to reproduce in us the character of Jesus - His love, His kindness, His compassion, His holiness, His humility, His unselfishness, His servant's spirit, His willingness to suffer wrongfully, His willingness to forgive. His character in us is what attracts the world to Him."

- Sharon White

CHAPTER 1

LOOKING BACK

It seems like only yesterday when Frank, my husband of twenty-four years (at the time), came home and told me casually in his thick Southern accent, "Oh, by the way, I have prostate cancer and the doctor wants to operate." I felt numb. *How could this be?*

Many things had happened in our lives, but never anything we couldn't handle. We thought we were "good" Christians who were able to release everything to God. But, this was just too much. The first thing that came to my mind was, "What about me and the kids." By now Vickie, our oldest, was grown and married. Willie, our son, was in a private university in New Orleans and Dorthy, our youngest daughter, was still at home, and a senior in high school.

Frank went on to say, "I knew a year ago that my PSA level was increasing but the doctor wanted to continue to watch it. Now he says it's at 5 and I have to do something about it."

"What! You knew a year ago and you didn't tell me!" I was angry! That happened a lot lately. I felt overwhelmed and stressed.

Frank was a quiet man that took life as it came. He was from the South with strong Christian values and work ethic. In his younger days, people would compare his looks to those of Billy Dee Williams. Working in a chemical company for many years helped keep him fit. Wisps of grey at his temples reflected his growing wisdom.

After working 28 years on a job he hated, Frank left and had taken a huge cut in pay. From there, he went on to work in another position that did not satisfy him. Finally, he decided enough was enough, and quit. Then we started a home-based business selling artwork and he was home full-time selling art and making frames. I was supportive of this arrangement until Frank dropped the bomb on me. Prostate cancer and no insurance except the policy my job provided. How were we going to manage?

I looked at my life. *There were entirely too many things going on.* After working all day at the college, I came home to entertain clients who had come over to buy art or frames. My living room had over 500 pictures in it and my dining room table was being used as a layout table for frames. My busy schedule had caused my eating habits to worsen and I was overweight. I tried to cover my graying hair several times but the grey still showed through. I felt old and tired. Our relationship seemed strained by the many pressures of life.

Finally, I said, "Frank, we need help. Something is not right. Let's go see Dr. Meyer." Dr. Meyer had been our marriage counselor in the past. He was a Christian counselor and we had not seen him in over three years. He had previously helped us see that our lifestyles had to change - and they had changed for the better. I'll never forget the visit to Dr. Meyer. He was a soft-spoken Christian psychologist who smiled all the time. He took the time to get to know you and treated you more like an invited guest than a paid client. Prior to seeing Dr. Meyer we had not sought counseling. Not that we didn't need it. We were just too proud to admit it.

On this visit Dr. Meyer seemed to be a different person. Yes, he was completely different. Instead of listening to our problems, Dr. Meyer started sharing an incident that happened to him that changed his life. At first I said to myself, "We're paying this man $120 an hour and he's telling us about his change. This is crazy!" Then something in me, I believe it was the Holy Spirit, told me to be quiet and listen.

Dr. Meyer started talking about how God had released him from triggers in his life that had affected his personality and beliefs. He talked for about 40 minutes. In the last 10 minutes of the conversation he said, "You know you don't need me. You need to go see Rev. Tilford in Middletown. Here's his number." We were definitely cautious. My husband asked, "What does he charge?" Dr. Meyer replied, "I don't think he charges anything. It's free!" FREE sounded good to me!

I have to admit, we would not have called Rev. Tilford if we had not seen the huge change in our psychologist. (We were also hurting so badly that we were desperate for anything that could help.) I remember the day I called Rev. Tilford. His answering machine picked up: "We're not in, leave a message." Secular music was playing in the background on his answering machine which I thought was odd. I dialed the number again and heard the same message.

Something was wrong. I did not have all the pieces of the puzzle. What I did know was that there was a prophet of God named Reverend Tilford that could solve all our problems. I knew the city where he lived, but that was all. I called information and there was no one by that name in the city. I called the surrounding cities. Nothing. I started calling the area churches. After the third church, a secretary knew the man and told me where his church was located and his first name.

Finally, I reached him. I must have transposed the number Dr. Meyer gave me, which was odd because as a math major, numbers were my livelihood. By the time I reached Reverend Tilford, my husband's surgery had been scheduled for the next week. Reverend

Tilford told me to call back after Frank felt better and he'd give us an appointment. In the meantime, he sent us a book to read about the process of healing: **<u>Genuine Recovery</u>** by Dr. Ed Smith.

The book was fascinating and included references for additional study. We ordered tapes and literature. To make a long story short, my husband had his surgery and God was very gracious to us.

I worked at a community college and each year I had nine weeks off. We had to schedule time off a year in advance. My husband's surgery was scheduled for Thursday and my last day of work was Tuesday. God had taken care of every detail. The surgery was a success, but we did not think so. Frank came home catheterized, wearing a bag that had to be emptied every few hours. I was so distressed. Lord, how could this be happening to us? I was home with Frank with nothing to do, but take care of him.

By now, you can probably guess that my husband was not use to anyone waiting on him. It was all I could do to keep him downstairs in the room I had prepared for him. After about 2 weeks, we were very bored. Frank was not well enough to go anywhere and he was still catheterized. To make the time go by faster, we started reading the literature Dr. Ed Smith sent us.

How could individuals who had been in bondage to sexual addiction, drug addiction, emotional trauma, rape, etc. receive healing so quickly? It just couldn't be. You see, we had an old image of God in a box and thought that He could only do things in the realm of our thinking. This book went way beyond what we had ever imagined. Frank and I became excited and could not wait to see Rev. Tilford. The third week after my husband's surgery, we scheduled a meeting with Tilford.

MEET REVEREND TILFORD

Reverend Tilford was a tall, stocky man with a quiet presence. He was a contractor turned Baptist minister. He was the picture of the classic country preacher, only needing the suspenders. I saw a peace and calmness in his eyes that I have never seen in any other minister. He was secure in his profession and it was clear to me that he really enjoyed the pies and cakes his congregation gave him.

I thought we would be going to a church where people prayed around you and where you would be delivered from internal demons that were causing you problems. Instead, Tilford greeted us at his front door and invited us in. Everything seemed strange. He did not know us and yet he said, "Sorry, I didn't hear the door bell, next time you can just walk in. We never lock our door."

Well, we went downstairs to his study and he said, "Who wants to go first?" I have always been the daring one in the family. I remembered that I had dragged my husband into this so I said, "I'll go first," I had everything planned. I knew God was going to heal me of a critical spirit and then it would be easier on my husband to have me around. The Lord had other plans. Rev. Tilford asked me a few questions then I prayed to myself. I kept thinking, "Oh no, he's going to start pulling out demons!"

You see, I had gone to another healing meeting before and I had never seen anything like it. People were rolling on the floor, laughing and foaming at the mouth, etc. I do believe some people were being healed, but I knew my intellect would not let me go there.

Instead, Rev. Tilford said, "Lord Jesus, take Sharon back to a memory, a thought, a place where she needs healing." Immediately I went back to my college years. I was 19 years old, a first-year student, and away from home for the first time. I met a man and fell in love with him. The next thing I knew, I became pregnant with his child. The man was married and tried to convince me to have an abortion! I was a preacher's daughter and I truly loved the Lord even at a young age. I struggled, "What should I do?" There was no one to advise me differently, so I had an abortion.

That was twenty-five years ago. For years, I had asked God for forgiveness, but I never felt forgiven, even though I knew God's grace was sufficient and that He had forgiven me. When Rev. Tilford took me back to that memory, I started to cry. It was more like a deep weeping with pain. I could see myself on the operating table. I felt the snip of the scissors. It was as if it was happening all over again. I then heard Rev. Tilford say that Christ was right there and that He was with me when it happened. Tilford prayed, "Lord Jesus, if it is Your will, have Sharon sense Your presence, see you, or hear what you have to say."

Suddenly, calmness came over me as I began to sense the presence of Jesus. He was right there with me! Not only was He there, but He also had my baby in His arms. He looked at me with a tender smile and I heard him say, "Sharon, I forgave you a long time ago and your baby is here with me." I saw my baby in His arms. I had never felt such joy and relief! It was as if a 25-year-old burden had been lifted from my shoulders. I heard the Reverend ask me to look around. "Is there anything else that bothers you about this picture?" How could I explain the overwhelming peace, joy and forgiveness…true forgiveness? I managed to say, "No, nothing." The Reverend was sensitive enough to leave me at this place of bliss. I could have stayed there forever. Then reality had to come.

WHAT IS THIS PROCESS?

Rev. Tilford started telling me a little about the process of healing. Through the Transformation Process, Jesus literally enters your past with you and heals you of the lies. Once Jesus heals you, you are healed.

Dr. Smith once said, and I paraphrase: "God did not tell the lame man in the Bible to go to the rehabilitation center and you will limp for the rest of your life." Most of us who have had any counseling or healing have experienced the rehabilitation route. He called this the tolerable recovery route. Jesus said, "Take up your bed and walk!" This is what Dr. Smith refers to as **Genuine Recovery**.

In this process, Jesus heals our past. What happened in the past does not change, but our interpretation of it does. Complete recovery will only come when Christ comes for His church. Until then, we must constantly renew our minds in Christ. This process teaches us how to do this on a daily basis. After going through the process, you can learn how to use it without a prayer-partner. Through Christ you can learn how to interpret your past. The way we interpret our past influences the way we see ourselves in the present. Jesus will take the lies and give us the truth.

He "has called you out of darkness into His wonderful light."
Peter 2:9

The lies of our past are like trees with branches. The branches represent the manifestations of the lies. You may cut off one branch at a time, but you have to kill the root to kill the tree. Once you kill the root of the tree, it will die. That is exactly how it is with this process. You kill the root of the lie, and the lie and its symptoms leave you forever. Without the lies of "shame, invalidation, abandonment, fear, hopelessness, confusion, powerlessness and unforgiveness," we are free to be all that God has called us to be.

As Rev. Tilford was explaining the healing process, I wasn't listening. I was still seeing Jesus holding my aborted child. I was sold on this healing process! All of this only took about 45 minutes. I learned that" God will meet you in your pain". He is with you in the darkness, cultivating in you a more mature faith and preparing you to receive a conqueror's crown.

Do I sound crazy? Yes, I know I do. Let me tell you a little something about myself. I mentioned that I worked at a community college. I had been an instructor there for 14 years. No, I didn't teach religion or philosophy. I taught computer programming. Before working for the school, I had worked for some top companies in our area, Proctor & Gamble and General Electric. I prided myself on my rational thinking and analytical mind. I was not the typical stereotype woman.

I had an undergraduate degree in mathematics and an MBA in business. This present experience was so different from my years of training and my beliefs. It didn't matter.

What mattered most was that I was healed of a wound that I didn't know I still had. The irony of it all is that even now when I go back to the scene of the abortion, I can see and feel Jesus holding my child. I can still feel His presence, his forgiveness and his joy. I came out of Rev. Tilford's room red-eyed and happy. Now it was Frank's turn.

FRANK'S STORY

When I found out I had cancer it was hard for me to swallow. I had never been ill before and I felt that I was going to die at age 55.

God sent someone to minister to me. She was a prayer warrior, the right person I needed to also help me. This lady was a realtor and a cancer survivor. She had undergone five surgeries for five different types of cancer. She was a living testimony. She taught me how to pray against the pain and to pray for victory in Jesus.

Before I went into surgery, I did exactly what my angel of mercy taught me and as a result, I experienced very little pain. After surgery, my wife had arranged for me to see Rev. Tilford. After 21 days, the doctor finally released me to leave the house, after which I went to see Rev. Tilford. I was angry with God. I wondered, "Why me? Why am I the only one with cancer!"

During the healing sessions with Rev. Tilford, he told me that I had to be willing to give up the anger I was carrying. God spoke to me and told me He still loved me. He took me back to the things I had been through in my life and showed me that every time, He was there for me.

I was grateful that I was alive, but more grateful that my wife and family stood by me when I needed them most. The first time I went through the process I had no idea what to expect, but I was willing to take the chance. There is a Proverbs that says: "If you want something you have never had, you must be willing to do something you have never done."

I had to be willing to go back to the pain, to the hurtful places in my life in order to be healed. That is when God took me through the healing of anger.

I did not go through just one session to deal with my anger, I went through five or six sessions with Rev. Tilford. Before the sessions, I was reluctant to tell anyone I had cancer, but after the sessions I was able to witness to many. I told every man who would listen about what happened to me. Some of the men went to the doctor to be tested themselves. You see, prostate cancer can be controlled and cured without surgery if you catch it in time.

I spent 2 years before surgery knowing that I had cancer and watching my PSA level increase. That was a real challenge for me. No matter how good I felt on a given day, Satan would come to me with accusations and get me to think thoughts as these: "Why are you so happy? You might be dead next year." I felt totally isolated and could not share this with my wife. The doctors had given me two choices - radiation or surgery.

One of the elders at the church wanted to lay his hands on me and pray for me. He told me God had healed me. At the time, I didn't understand what he meant, but now I do. Not only did God heal me of cancer, but he healed my spirit also. The doctors found out after surgery that all of the cancer had been removed.

God released me from my anger and gave me peace. After meeting with Rev. Tilford, I later began to attend the classes to learn more about the healing process. The healing process truly changed my life, but it also gave me the ability to look at a person's spirit rather than their flesh. I now can thank God for any situation in my life. If it had not been for the cancer, I would not have been delivered.

A MINISTRY IS BORN

After seeing Tilford, Frank and I knew we could not leave him without giving him a love offering. Frank and I calculated that a psychologist costs about $100 an hour. We thought we should at least give him half of that. He had seen Frank and me for approximately 90 minutes. We only had $100 on us so gave him what we had. We felt like new babes in Christ.

"Therefore if any man be in Christ, he is a new creature: old things are passed away; behold, All things are become new"
2 Corinthians 5:17

After the first meeting with Rev. Tilford, Frank and I knew we would never be the same. How could we be the same? God had done work on us that we just couldn't describe. We were both shell-shocked. We drove the forty-five minutes home in silence not believing what had happened. I kept wondering, "Will I feel this joy and peace tomorrow? Is this a temporary reaction?" I knew I had to go back. I wanted more. A seed was planted in our hearts that day and a ministry was born.

CHAPTER 2

GOING BACK FOR MORE HEALING

During my second visit with Reverend Tilford's, I met his wife Cindy. She was a delight. Cindy was a tiny little lady that looked like a college student. She had short cropped hair that blew with the wind. Cindy was always busy chatting and smiling. She appeared to be the opposite of her very calm, quiet husband. I felt as if I had seen her somewhere before but I couldn't figure out where. When Tilford took me into his study, he mentioned that his wife was a survivor and then it struck me. She was on the videotape from Dr. Ed Smith.

Cindy had allowed herself to be videotaped while Dr. Smith was taking her through the healing process. I thought, "What courage!" If she needed healing so badly that she was bold enough to show the world the process on video, I knew Dr. Smith's methods would work for me too.

CAN CHRISTIANS HAVE DEMONS?

That day, Tilford kept me for over an hour and we discovered I did indeed have demons. Yes, I am a born-again believer. I had been reading several books on deliverance that suggested that a born-again Christian cannot have demons. THIS IS NOT TRUE!

"And this woman, <u>a daughter of Abraham</u> as she is, whom Satan has bound for eighteen years, should she not have been released from this bondage on the Sabbath day." Luke 13:16

Reverend Tilford used Dr. Smith's process to bind the spirits in me and cast them out. Oddly, while going through the process, I wanted to laugh. Isn't that odd? Everything Rev. Tilford did was authentic. No, I didn't foam at the mouth, roll around on the floor, scream, laugh, or yell. He commanded the demons not to speak and then he forbade them to physically manifest in the name of Jesus.

DELIVERANCE IS MINE

In that hour-long process, I was delivered from the hatred of housework. Yes, I HATED HOUSEWORK! Housework did not make sense to me. You did it over and over again, but the house would still be a mess a few days later. I remember God took me back to a memory of me as a baby. I was a fat, cute, bow-legged baby that craved adult attention. My mother had left me at another lady's home that was filled with clutter. Somehow the need for clutter set in on me at that time. God then healed me from the need for clutter. That day I came home and cleaned my basement. Now, let me tell you about our basement! Our basement was the place we kept our frame-making equipment (for our art gallery) along with our normal household clutter. We had over 300 pieces of molding scattered across the floor. Everything was covered with sawdust, wood and metal chips from cutting frames. There was no ventilation in our basement - it really was a fire hazard.

Linda, my girlfriend's daughter, was an artist who worked part-time with us in the framing business. She was a strong believer in God, but doubted the healing process. I had tried to convince her many times to just try it, but she refused. Linda hated our basement. The next day, at a retirement party for Linda's mother, I told Linda that there was some work I needed for her to do at the house. I knew she would have to see it to believe it.

I couldn't wait to surprise her. When she walked into the basement, she could hardly believe her eyes. It was a completely different place. Linda became a believer of the healing process that day!

"Wow! I can believe!"

WHEN GOD HEALS YOU OF YOUR PAST IT MAKES A CHANGE IN YOUR PRESENT

The change that occurred in me caused me to finally feel worthy of having things that I could afford and enabled me to free my life of clutter.

Then I went to work on the upstairs. I had a sofa in the living room that my mother had re-upholstered twenty years ago. The springs had completely given out. The other furniture had been purchased at garage sales over the years. The place was a mess!

Linda was a gifted interior designer so I sent her shopping for me. She purchased new sofas, chairs, tables, and other things. My living space changed dramatically. What was a horribly embarrassing room became a grand parlor. Why had it taken me twenty years to fix it up? Was it money? No. Was it time? No.

During that second session with Rev. Tilford, not only was I healed from the need for clutter, I was also healed from feeling unworthy. Even though I made a good salary, I did not feel worthy enough to own new furniture. I felt I didn't deserve it. Yes, God healed me. Surely, if I'm an heir through Christ, he would expect me to have decent furniture!

He allowed me to understand Romans 8:17. It reads:

"Now if we are children, then we are heirs - heirs of God and co-heirs with Christ..." Romans 8:17

WHO CAN I PRACTICE ON?

By this time, I wanted everyone to know about this ministry. Frank and I had watched all the videotapes, read the training materials and were ready to try the healing on someone. The author claimed that the process was so simple, that even we could do it. God speaks to all of us! This process just taught us how to listen.

Who could I try this on? My two sisters thought I was crazy and wanted no part of it. My youngest daughter, Dorthy was old enough to say no and mean it. My sister Terry was a single parent raising her daughter, Tammy. Tammy was only ten years old and had gone through a lot of trauma in her young life. Tammy was coming to spend the weekend with us.

Tammy was a sweet, easy-going child with an accommodating personality and loved to please adults. I asked her if she would let me practice on her. "Tammy, I need someone to practice on. Will you let me take you through a healing process? I promise it won't hurt you." She replied, "Okay, Aunt Sharon, what do I have to do? Just relax baby and I'm going to ask Jesus to come into your life and take you to where you need healing." I began, "Lord Jesus speak to Tammy. Take her to a memory of where she needs to be healed." Immediately, Tammy started to cry. I asked, "Where are you?" She replied, "I'm at Mema's house." Mema was my mother. Tammy lived with Mema for three years. During that time, Mema became ill and had grown progressively worse. She was finally diagnosed with Dementia.

"What's happening baby?" I asked. "Mema is talking on the telephone and telling her friend that I took her money. I didn't take her money." Tammy cried. I asked her, "How old are you?" She said that she was eight years old. I told Tammy that Jesus was right there with her and she opened her eyes. I asked her, "What's happening now?" She said, "I see Jesus standing over there." I asked if she wanted to go to him, she said yes. I told her to go to him and tell me what he was doing. She said, "He's holding me and saying '"Hush little baby don't you cry.'" I prayed, "Lord Jesus, is there anything else you want to say to Tammy?" Tammy then told me that Jesus said that her grandmother was ill and that she wouldn't be living there much longer. I continued to pray, "Lord, speak the truth to Tammy." Tammy began to cry again saying, "I see Jesus on his knees in front of God turning Mema over to God. He told me it will be okay and that Mema would be okay." After this process, I asked Tammy how she felt. She said that she felt good and that she thanked God for healing her.

At this point I stopped the process. I was in tears. I thought, "Poor Tammy... Poor Mema... Poor Me!" Deep inside I felt I had been on Holy Ground. Jesus had let me share in an experience that healed Tammy. Thank you Lord for the healing!

"No eye has seen, no ear has heard, no mind has conceived what God has prepared for those who love him - but God has revealed it to us by His Spirit." 1 Corinthians 2:9-10

I was ready now! I had seen the process work. I knew the Lord had given me this ministry. So, I started telling everyone my story.

Melvin, a friend of my son, was having emotional problems. He was extremely bright and graduated at the top of his class. Every year around February and March, he would experience a great depression that made it difficult for him to get out of bed.

I asked my daughter to mention the process to him. She didn't mention it. I imagine she felt it was bad enough having her mother running around telling all her personal business. She surely wasn't about to get any of her friends or my son's friends involved.

One day I had the chance to talk to Melvin and asked him if he would go to Reverend Tilford's with me. He agreed. I set up an appointment and we were off to Rev. Tilford. I asked Melvin if it was all right for me to sit in. Although Melvin agreed, Reverend Tilford told me that if Melvin became uncomfortable, I would have to leave. That seemed fair to me. I felt that I was now an apprentice. My years of teaching helped me learn quickly from Reverend Tilford.

Tilford began Melvin's healing by addressing Melvin's battle with depression. God took Melvin back to the memories of his childhood. He remembered having a floor pallet next to his mother's bed. He had witnessed his father fall onto his pallet and die. He was two years old and found this very confusing.

During the process, Jesus spoke to Melvin and held him. Melvin heard Jesus say that he was not alone and that He would be there for him. Melvin spoke of the safety of being in Jesus' arms. By the end of Melvin's session, I was in tears again. Jesus healed Melvin from the haunting memories of his early childhood.

Melvin talked a mile a minute on the drive back to Cincinnati, "I can't wait to see my mother and tell her that I'm sorry for the way I treated her. She's been so good to me all these years." Melvin told me that he had blamed his mother for his father's death. After his father's death, Melvin never got close to his mother and their relationship was estranged.

What can I say? This has to be the work of Jesus. Who else could change a person's heart overnight?

"For I will restore you to health and I will heal you of your wounds, saith the Lord." Jeremiah 30:17

OPEN FOR BUSINESS

If I could, I would have hung a shingle on our door and opened up for business that day. God was gracious to me and only sent people to me who were not severely damaged. I found it interesting that nearly all of the women that God sent to me had had an abortion. Most of the men that came were addicted to sex and had engaged in pornography, homosexuality or adultery.

In the early stages of our ministry, I was still very damaged in many ways. I was immature and hasty. People would often call for healing and set up a time to meet and then not show up. I remember during the Christmas holidays; nine people didn't show up! After this, I began to make rules. If someone scheduled a time to meet and did not show, I asked them to give $30 to the church's benevolent fund. I don't know why people didn't show up. I might have been a no-show too.

I remember chasing down one of our church's Elders. "Hey Jerry, you have to come and see what I am doing," I remarked.

He said he would come on Tuesday at 6:00 p.m. Tuesday came and there was no Jerry. I called his home and left a message on his answering machine. He didn't show up. Jerry was a young professional who owned his own business. $30 would not have made any difference in his finances. He just didn't know how to tell me no. When I saw him at church, I made a beeline to him. "Jerry, why didn't you show up?" "Oh, I forgot," was his reply. I guess he thought I was crazy when I told him the he had one more chance.

We rescheduled for the following Tuesday. Tuesday came and again, Jerry did not show. I finally got the message, but I was not healed enough to just leave Jerry alone. After church, I cornered Jerry again. "Jerry, you owe the church $30 for standing me up!" I said. "Okay Sharon, put me down for Tuesday again," he replied. This time Jerry showed up and so did Jesus! Just imagine! I was running people down trying to heal them.

"YOU NEED TO BE HEALED!"

These were my first experiences with this healing method. Obviously, I went about it incorrectly. My own methods needed readjusting. In hindsight, I realize that God had everything in his hands. His plan was being accomplished.

"So then that ye walk circumspectly not as fools; but as wise, redeeming the time because the days are evil." Ephesians 5:15-16

THERE'S ALWAYS ROOM TO GROW

It was about this time when Frank and I decided to close the framing business for ten weeks while he recuperated from surgery. It was during this time that I moved the pictures from the living room and gave our designer, Linda, an opportunity to decorate the house.

I also realized that I no longer wanted a frame shop in our house. My beautiful new furniture just wouldn't go with all those frames. I told Frank about my feelings and he suggested that we pray about it. "If God wants us to have a shop and move the business, he'll provide one for us." Over the years I had grown to admire my husband's wisdom, knowledge and discernment.

I remember telling Frank that I would love to have a shop in Wyoming. Wyoming was a well-manicured, affluent neighborhood whose residents boasted incomes of $400,000 and over. The CEO of Cincinnati's largest employer lived in Wyoming. The residents seemed to be loyal to their community. Many of them bought homes there and remained until they died, and their next generation did the same.

I grew up in Glendale, a neighborhood similar to Wyoming. The rich lived on one side of the tracks, and everyone else lived on the other. As kids, we all went to school together, played together and bonded with each other.

My father was an associate minister at a church. In those days this was not a paid position, so he also worked for General Electric as a machinist and helped fix cars in the neighborhood. My mother was a homemaker and helped make ends meet by sewing our clothes and baby-sitting, Because no one told us differently, we believed that we were as rich as the kids on the other side of the tracks.

My sister Brenda owned a travel agency in Wyoming. After being at that location for nine years, her landlord decided to rent to someone else. Brenda was desperately looking for a new place and had only a month to relocate.

The night after Frank and I prayed about moving the business, I received a call from Brenda. "Sharon, there's a building in Wyoming that has been up for rent for the last two months. It's too small for me. Maybe you and Frank can use it for the shop."

Even though, Frank and I believe in the power of prayer, the way God always comes through still amazes me. Brenda gave me the landlord's phone number. Frank called Mr. Sears, the landlord, and after their conversation, we both thanked God for the blessing we knew would come. We both felt that this would be our new place of business.

Mr. Sears was a delight. He was a born-again Christian and he and his wife loved the Lord. He showed us the rental space. It was small and cozy, comprised of three rooms. We would only need to knock a few walls out, paint and carpet the place. The rent was within the amount Frank and I prayed for, Mr. Sears was exactly the type of landlord we prayed for, and the location was in the exact area we prayed for. We rented the place immediately.

"Ask and it will be given to you; seek and you will find; knock and the door will be opened to you. For everyone who asks receives; he who seeks finds; and to him who knocks, the door will be opened."
Matthew 7:7-8

Frank was still recovering from his operation and the doctor had removed the catheter. Frank is the calm and sensible one in the family. He is rarely upset or excited.

Well, the day we signed the lease, Frank was excited. The very next day, against my wishes, he went to the shop. He designed his workspace, determined how much inventory he needed, and behaved like a kid with a new toy. Frank was under doctor's orders not to lift anything. How could I keep him from working on the shop?

Along came Lou. Lou was different. I had never met a man with so many talents who lacked the ability to use them effectively. He looked something like a wild lion with blonde hair that needed a good combing. He had blue eyes that seemed to be on fire. If you saw Lou on the street you would think he was insane and probably pass by on the other side. Lou was a gentle as a lamb. He and Frank got along perfectly. Lou had the skill of three men. He became Frank's hands and in four weeks, the shop was ready for us to move in.

" Hi I am LOU!"

It was beautiful! We dedicated the shop to the Lord and agreed to only use it for his purposes. We christened the shop, "The Frank White Gallery and Frame Shop," and Frank moved in. Praise God! Even the smallest details of our lives were arranged by God! I had my home back and my husband now had a shop.

"Giving thanks always for all things unto God and the Father in the name of our Lord Jesus Christ." Ephesians 5:20

CHAPTER 3

MINISTERING AT WORK

By now, I was back at work. I did not fully understand the scripture that states, "We are in the world, but not of the world" until I returned to work.

My church members referred to me as the "crazy" deliverance person who happened to be the pastor's sister. Yes, at this time I was attending my brother's church. I did not let that sway me. I was more determined to continue the healing ministry. I decided to work on the instructors at the college.

In those days I still had a lot of growing up to do. I know now that I should have prayed and asked God to lead me to the people He wanted me to work with. Even though I prayed that prayer, I felt that I needed to help God out.

If you've never worked in a collegiate environment, you would have a difficult time understanding the mentality of teachers, especially college professors. Most of my colleagues were highly skilled and could demand twice their salary somewhere else. These were people who loved to teach. They were in total control of their classrooms. Professors set the standard and determine who passes and who fails.

A college gathers many intellectuals with many viewpoints and puts them in one location. In an atmosphere like this, there is often no room for God or His Son, Jesus. It would be almost inconceivable that these professors would give up control and allow someone else - an invisible someone else to determine their future.

No way! Many of these intellectuals were admitted atheists or agnostics.

Now mind you, I had been a teacher for 18 years and I knew that religion was a subject that was discussed and argued about, but never taken too seriously. At the college, it was like having a conversation about any other topic of interest.

CAN INTELLECTUALS BE HEALED?

Knowing all this, I was still undaunted. I thought that since the church was not responsive to my healing ministry, God must have opened up the college for my ministry. *Well, it made sense at the time.* There were so many hurting people on campus and I felt that God had sent me to heal every one of them.

Shortly after returning to work I was selected to attend a conference in Nashville with two of my colleagues. At this time, my son Willie was at home from college and had noticed a great change in Frank and me.

Willie was born-again and serious about the Lord. He immediately made an appointment with Reverend Tilford and received healing. My husband, Frank had his hands full with the shop so I asked Willie to drive me to Nashville for the conference. While at the conference, Ted, my co-worker of 15 years, went beyond an unspoken boundary and came onto my territory.

I was responsible for two computer programs. I was teaching three classes a day and advising over 300 students. Ted saw me at dinner. He and Jim were there and I knew something was up. Ted was my program chair. The program chair is the person who assigns the instructors' their classes. Over the years we had become friends and respected each other. Ted knew I liked to have my lunch hour open so he would give me a 9:00 class, a 10:00 class and then maybe a 1:00 or 2:00 class. He also knew the classes I enjoyed teaching and would designate those to me. I had already approached Ted about my new mission in life and he dismissed it as just a phase I was going through.

At dinner Ted said, "Sharon, I've decided to give one of your programs to Jim and let him advise the students. You are advising way too many students. You can keep the other one." I thought, "How dare he?" I was angry that he would take the program that I had built from scratch and give it to someone else.

At this point, I had already received over 10 hours of healing with Reverend Tilford. I did not feel intimidated or powerless. For the first time in my life, I stood up to Ted. I looked him straight in the eye and said, "No, Ted. You're not taking my program. I am no longer going to advise any students. You can have both programs and all advising." Jim almost fainted. I imagine he had never seen anyone talk to the program chair that way!

"Yes, I am clueless to the things of God!"

I knew that I was in for a fight. Ted was brilliant, a Mensa. He was one of those quiet geniuses with an astronomical IQ, but spiritually blind. Only one tenth of one percent of the world's population has Mensa genius. Ted did not cause any problems at the conference. I guess he thought that I would change my mind later. I didn't!

When we arrived from Nashville, the word had gotten around our group that I had stood up to Ted. One of my co-workers, Gus, a believer, was tickled. We both knew that Ted was not a believer that we felt that God had put him in our path to disciple him.

In hindsight, Ted was right. I did have too many students and too much work. I was not healed enough to accept the change.

Ted is the type of man that never loses, especially when he is right. After I didn't back down, I received a call from Ted's boss, but that didn't matter.

I had never been so bold in all my life. I always went along and agreed with everything. Not anymore! God had given me the boldness of a lion - He had not created, but rather 'delivered' a MONSTER!

I did not realize at the time that God was moving items from my plate so that I would have time for the ministry. Only teaching and not advising students freed up at least 20 hours of my time each week.

For every action there is a reaction. The following school term I got the worst schedule I had ever had in my life. I had an 8:00 class, a 12:00 class and a night class! Ted scheduled me on Bible study night. I hadn't taught nights in years. I knew I had to make peace with Ted, but how? The only way I thought it could be possible was by prayer and encouraging Ted to see Reverend Tilford.

Before my healing, I would have been angry with Ted. I would never have felt as if I could make a difference. After being healed I no longer felt powerless. God was in control of my life.

By now, I was a regular at the Tilford home. I knew his grandchildren and daughter-in-law. I felt very much at home there. I would take anyone I could to Tilford and watch him take them through the process. I had learned so much and had actually taken about 30 people through the process myself.

The Reverend started a class for those of us who wanted more training. He also encouraged me to see Dr. Ed Smith, the inventor of this process. I felt that I needed to go because I was hitting a brick wall with some of the people, but I did not want to go to Campbellsville, Kentucky by myself.

Frank's business started to take off after moving into the shop. Although he supported the healing ministry, he felt his focus was to be on the administrative end. He was an elder at the church and the church was growing. His time was very limited. Whenever a male came for healing; however, Frank was always there to cover me. I learned from Reverend Tilford that one should never underestimate the enemy and that I should not have a man in the house for healing, unless someone else was present.

"Abstain from all appearance of evil." 1 Thessalonians 5:22

MEETING DR. ED SMITH

I told my pastor about my personal need to go see Dr. Smith. The church board met and I received $900 plus travel expenses to make the journey. Frank drove me to the beautiful
Alathia Equipping Center Chalet, situated in the middle of nowhere.
The Center had swimming pools, spring water and acres upon acres of trails and forests. The facility held 33 people and was divided into sections for couples, and singles. We were greeted that night with a wonderful home-cooked meal and later met our presenter and educator, Dr. Ed. Smith.

To attend these sessions, it is required that you have seen at least 20 people, gone through the videos and read the training manual. Although I had seen over thirty people, watched the videos twice and read the manual three times, I was still unprepared for what I would learn there.

The first night was preliminary. We fellowshipped and met Dr. Smith. Dr. Smith was a clinical psychologist. He had a thick head of black hair and dark eyes. He could have been Italian or Greek if he hadn't been wearing those tell-tell Kentucky "cowboy boots." He drove up in a pick-up truck and all he needed was a pair of guns and a horse to complete his outfit.

He shared the rules for our adventure in learning. There were only two lay people there, myself and another man. I was fascinated by the varied religious groups and denominations represented there. There were Messianic Jews, Protestants, Catholics, members of the Church of the Nazarene, Baptists, Church of God In Christ, and Pentecostals in attendance. There were people from all over the country and the globe. I even met a couple from South Africa. Ninety percent of the people there were in full-time ministry or psychologists. Thank God for my healing! Had I not been healed; I would have felt out of place in this group.

Yes, these were working sessions. Dr. Smith proved to be an exceptionally hardworking teacher, and the Master of this healing process given to him by God. He expected his students to work as well. We awoke at 8:00 a.m. and went to bed at 10:00 p.m. Breakfast was both optional and self-prepared. Praise and worship began at 8:00 a.m.

Dr. Smith began his presentations at 9:00 a.m. I had two roommates, Dorothy and Mary. Dorothy was in full- time ministry and lived solely on donations. I said to myself, "What faith she must have!" Mary was a social worker who owned a business that employed eight psychologists. Since learning the process, she and her staff had been booked 10 hours a day, 6 days a week. I couldn't wait for the presentations to begin.

I had never been to a conference with only ministry people. It was great to see persons of various denominations all singing and praising God together. The conference attendees sounded like a professional choir. I was amazed at the voices in the room. It later dawned on me that many of these people were probably worship leaders in their congregations. I recall that when our church was first planted, the pastor and his wife ran all aspects of the church, including the music.

I learned so much at the first day's sessions, I was ready to go HOME. The training was intense. Dr. Smith gave us so much to learn in a short period of time. In just three years, Dr. Smith's ministry had been replicated in over 45 states and 25 nations. It seemed that the whole world was seeking healing.

The Center, managed by Dr. Smith's family, ran excellently. The food was terrific. After the first day, I knew that this was much deeper than I had ever believed. We were dealing with the enemy and the enemy was upset. Dr. Smith warned us that things would happen during the sessions to distract us.

My roommate Mary received a call advising her that two of her clients had committed suicide. Another pastor received word that three of his members died in an auto accident. We prayed for them and continued to press on.

By 7:00 p.m. we were all very tired. We still had to complete our homework assignments so we broke off into small groups of three and practiced healing techniques. I was paired with a pastor's wife who was a Messianic Jew and a Presbyterian pastor who had not been through the healing process at all.

Later that night I spoke of this pastor with my roommate. I realized how important it is for pastors and leaders to appear "healed." Who could they trust with their innermost secrets? Mary told me of a pastor she knew who would cross five states to come to her for healing so that no one in his congregation or immediate circle would know.

I had formerly been guilty of putting pastors and clergy on a pedestal. I realize now that they are human beings just like the rest of us. It is unfortunate that many of them are not afforded the luxury of receiving healing. I thank God that I'm a lay-person.

"...If any man thirst, let him come unto me and drink." John 7:37

CHAPTER 4

HEALING FOR MY FAMILY

After I returned from Dr. Smith's training class, I was overwhelmed, but ready to do God's will. I'd learned some basic skills that most counselors take for granted and more than I really wanted to know about healing. My roommate, Mary, taught me to take a person only so far in the healing process at a given time to avoid making them totally transparent.

When I took Dorthy through the process, God led her through six memories in less than 40 minutes. Mary admonished me to never take a person through that much trauma on their first time. She compared that to stripping a person naked and sending them out into the world. It would be difficult to recover without first having built a trusting relationship with the person. Then I realized what huge mistakes I had make on about 30 people.

There were some people came to me for healing and never came back. I never understood why until then. I had formerly encouraged them to go from one memory to the next. It really was too much, too soon.

I learned the value of taking a person through only a few memories at a time. I also learned the value of having intercessory prayer covering during times of ministry. Although my husband had been my spiritual covering, I really needed an intercessor at each session, praying for the person and for me.

Barb was the only intercessor I could think of who did not think that I was crazy. She was a young woman I met through the art business. She had a heart for the Lord and her calling was prayer. She had been one of my first cases. Spiritually, I stripped her naked and sent her home as well. She never came back. I called Barb and asked if she would be willing to pray during my sessions. She agreed.

At this time, I had appointments from 4:00 p.m. to 10:00 p.m. every Monday and Tuesday. I could always tell that Barb and Frank were praying. I would often call Barb after a session and say, "I know you were praying because there was so much healing." Barb always came through. I arranged to call Barb after my sessions so that she could stop praying. A few times I was so tired that I went to sleep without calling her and she prayed all night!

After many of our sessions, Frank would go from room to room cleaning our home of any residue that may have been left during the session. What is residue, you ask? Before being called into this ministry, I would have thought this was preposterous. Yes, demons can linger in a person's home.

In fact, we'll never forget the night that our daughter Dorthy, who was 18 at the time, woke up saying, "Mom, Dad, there is someone outside my window!" We both went to her room and heard chanting, singing and hissing. It was definitely human. Frank began to pray and Dorthy and I followed suit. Suddenly, a loud hissing sound and a cat cry followed, then silence.

Dorthy slept in the chair in our bedroom that night. The next day Frank and I walked around the house and he cleansed the outside of the house just like he had cleansed the inside.

PRAISE THE LORD FOR MIRACLES!

I prayed a long time for my daughter Dorthy to go through the healing process. I petitioned God like the widow in the Scriptures petitioned the judge. (Luke 18) Dorthy was a senior in high school and God had given her a gift of music. She'd played the viola since she was six years old and it was her major.

Dorthy became very serious about her music at age 17 and began to surpass her peers. She played beautifully for her teacher and for her parents, but there was one really tragic flaw. She suffered from stage fright. It is impossible for a professional musician to earn a living with stage fright. When her teacher demanded that she have a senior recital, Dorthy was on pins and needles about it. I kept asking her if she would go through the process, but she flatly refused.

During the morning after she heard the noises outside her window, God answered my prayers. Dorthy shyly came to me and asked to know more about the healing process. I informed her that one of the people I had seen that night had a grandfather who was a witch. It was the witch that we heard singing. Dorthy asked to be taken through the process. Praise God!

"I love to play in front of folks!"

That day, Dorthy was completely healed of stage fright. She played in front of over 200 people for her viola recital. Next, she volunteered to play at her school's graduation where over 1,000 people attended. Thank you Jesus for miracles!

"And we know that in all things God works for the good of those who love him, who have been called according to his purpose."
Romans 8:28

At this point, I no longer went to Reverend Tilford for healing. I had learned to hear God's voice on my own. Frank and I had been healed and were able to perform the process on each other. Imagine that! After being married for twenty-four years, we were each other's past and each other's triggers. So at least once a month, we would take each other through the process. I began to learn so much about the man I married. I began to understand his fears, his pain, and his joy. We were finally transparent with each other.

I kept praying for Dorthy to come back for healing but she didn't for a long time. God is so gracious! I had not received healing until I was 46 years old. She was only 18. I could easily be patient. She was already 30 years ahead of me.

Our oldest daughter, Vickie, was married and had two sons, Michael and Emmanuel. She and her husband Deon were Christians. Deon had come from a Pentecostal background and deliverance was the rule, not the exception. I told them both about the ministry and asked them to go through the process. Vickie came, but did not receive any healing. I continued to pray for them.

Deon and Vickie announced at Dorthy's recital they would be transferring to Rhode Island. Rhode Island? Where is that? It seemed like the other side of the world. Our daughter and our grandchildren were going to be leaving. I thank God that Frank and I were healed enough to accept their decision without giving our advice.

The move was very traumatic for Vickie and Deon. Vickie had never been away from home. She attempted to go to Ohio State University in Columbus, Ohio, but she didn't like it. She liked structure and the familiar. She did not handle change very well.

I casually asked Deon for the 100th time if he and Vickie wanted to go through the process. To my surprise, this time they said yes. I learned a lot from my son-in-law the day he showed up for healing. Although he believed that God could heal him of anything, it was difficult for him to believe that God could use me to do it. I praise God that their healing had nothing to do with me. Jesus showed up and healed them both.

In hindsight, I believe I now know why it was hard for my church members to come to me for healing. I was the preacher's sister, a believer and a lover of the Lord. I was also arrogant, critical of everything and everybody and I had a disagreeable spirit. Why would any of them, having known me, come to me for anything-especially healing? Unfortunately, they knew me then; now, my whole life had changed. I was in the process of being healed...

Thank goodness God does not require perfection for His people. Thank goodness for God's grace! Paul says it so clearly in I Timothy 1:13-16:

"Even though I was a blasphemer and a persecutor and a violent man, I was shown mercy because I acted in ignorance and unbelief. The grace of our Lord was poured out on me abundantly, along with the faith and love that are in Christ Jesus. Here is a trustworthy saying that deserves full acceptance: Christ Jesus came into the world to save sinners –of whom I am the worst. But for that very reason I was shown mercy so that in me, the worst of sinners, Christ Jesus might display his unlimited patience as an example for those who would believe on him and receive eternal life." 1 Timothy 1:13-16

My son, Willie was in New Orleans, Louisiana. He had left campus living and was worshipping with a local church. It was a small church plant with a very young minister. Willie was rooming with a friend in one of the minister's apartments. He slept on the floor next to a six-foot long boa constrictor.

"Hey Mom meet my roommate!"

Willie stated that he did not want any furniture that he could not leave with the church. Frank and I were concerned and decided to go to New Orleans to visit. At this point, I knew my son needed healing. While in New Orleans, the minister's wife received a tremendous amount of healing and wanted Willie to learn the process. Willie came home at Christmas-time.

We spent more than 40 hours in training. He had previously learned how to do the process on himself and now he needed to practice. Like I had done early on, he practiced on Tammy. Willie was well learned and did an excellent job. He was 21 years old, invincible, and a warrior for the Lord.

I was still within the nine-week term at the college, teaching on Wednesday nights, but now that I was not advising students, my work was easy. My entire workgroup was estranged from me. I was not invited to meetings, I was left out of decision-making and I didn't even get E-mails. LIFE WAS WONDERFUL! All I had to do was teach my two classes during the day and my one class at night.

God put such a need in Ted's life - he finally went to see Reverend Tilford. When he returned I knew he would never be the same. He gave up the program chair position and finally had time to get involved in the things he liked doing: learning new software and developing curriculum. My next classes were scheduled from 9:00 a.m. - 11:00 a.m. This was a great schedule. I had three classes per week, eight office hours and the rest of the time was my own. How could I ask for more?

My marriage was better than ever. The process allowed both Frank and me to grow up and mature in Christ. God seemed to erase all the years of bad times and truly redeemed the time. God had given us so much. The Scripture tells us that to whom much is given, much is required.

I was booked solid. I was giving 12 to 16 hours a week to the ministry. The types of cases I was seeing had changed dramatically. The majority of my former female clients had been sexually abused, raped or had an abortion. The men were generally coping with some type of sexual addiction.

Now it seemed that most of my clients were disassociated and victims of sexual rituals. Most of these persons had been in professional counseling for at least five years and were now coming to me. One pastor sent his entire congregation to me, one member at a time. I thank God that they were able to receive healing. In fact, most of his members were the type of clients that a professional would need to see.

Although I felt blessed to be serving the Lord, it was becoming increasingly difficult to buy literature, books, and videos to supplement the healing ministry. Once, when Frank was taking me through the healing process, God spoke to me saying, "You have not because you ask not." After that point, I began to mention to my clients that we would appreciate a donation for ministry costs. Praise the Lord! The people did not give much but God increased the net worth of our business.

Now that I have been operating the ministry for more than a year, I can look back on my life and witness that God does indeed heal the broken-hearted. A year has gone by so fast it seems more like 20 years. So many people have gone through the process and received healing.

I want you to understand that healing is a process! We must renew our minds constantly. Dr. Ed Smith has just come up with a systematic way for lay people to learn how to bring about this healing process.

In his book, **<u>Sins of the Father</u>**, W. Worley said it so plainly, "For we are more than conquerors", but we must continue to keep the grass mowed and pull up the tree stumps until Jesus comes again.

CHAPTER 5

HEALING FOR MY CHURCH FAMILY

After returning from Dr. Smith's training, our pastor asked Frank and me to teach a relationship class at the church. I had been involved in over 120 hours of healing, but only four of our church members had been through the process.

The more our pastor promoted the class to the congregation, the more Frank and I prayed. We had 13 people show up for the first session. It was to be a two hour class, on Monday evenings for eight weeks. Having a private session with Frank and me was one of the requirements of the class.

I will never forget the first night of class. As I stated before, I have been teaching adults for over 15 years. For some reason, I experienced a great deal of fear. I was accustomed to giving grades to students who took my class. This however, was a volunteer class of people who would be grading me. These were people who knew me as Sharon, the pastor's sister, not Sharon, the teacher.

Frank and I prayed before class and he took me through the process. God spoke to me and said:
1. This is not your class, it is my class.
2. I sent you to teach this class.
3. You have everything you need.
4. I will be there with you.
5. You cannot fail.

That made all the difference to me. I was ready!

That night I introduced the process, shared some of my history with the process, explained the rules and asked for a volunteer. No one volunteered. Thank God for Frank! He agreed to go through the healing process.

My husband Frank is a very quiet and humble man. He was respected in the church as a worker and a lover of the Lord. He was very reserved and few people really knew him. He was not the type of person to readily be transparent. For Frank to allow me to take Him through the healing process in front of the group was a clear indication to me that he had been healed. Frank's healing that night broke the ice and gave the class credibility. After that, all but one gentleman scheduled an appointment for a private session. The class was a success!

At the second class we watched a video on prayer and I took the whole group through the process. Working with a group is just like working with an individual. When God takes someone in the group to a specific memory, I simply have them raise their hand. When Jesus speaks to someone in the group, they had the option of writing it on paper or verbalizing it. That evening, about two-thirds of the class received healing. The others were scheduled for one-on-one sessions during the week.

JESUS HEALS THEM ALL

After being a member of the same church for many years, Frank and I joined another church where I served as an altar worker. When people go to the altar, they are usually in desperate need of receive healing or a Word from God. Quiet as kept, I used the healing process at the altar on Sunday. I have seen hundreds of hurting people received healing at the altar through this ministry. Jesus truly does HEAL THEM ALL!

God gave us favor and we became leaders of the church care team. This team is actually responsible for going to funerals, taking care of the needs of the members, and hospital visits, representing our church.

One funeral in particular stood out for us. When Frank and I arrived at the funeral home we were surprised to see about 200 young people from 15 to 19 years old. Upon greeting the family, we understood why so many young people were in attendance. The deceased person was only 17 years old. He was killed in a gang related shooting. What do you say to a mother who has lost her 17 year old child? What words of comfort come to you? As we greeted the family, we saw a 9-year-old girl sitting, rocking, and weeping.

Frank asked her, "Was this your brother?" She said, through her tears, "Yes, he was my brother."

I asked the girl's mother if we could pray for her. Her mother consented. "Lord Jesus, Mary needs a word from you today. Speak to her heart, Lord. She needs a word of comfort." Mary stopped crying and looked at us. She said, "My brother is going to be alright." "What else Lord does she need to know?" Mary said, "He will see me again." Frank asked the mother had he given his life to Christ. The child's mother said, "Yes, just last week." Praise God, HE is always on time. After that Mary told us that Jesus was rocking her saying, "Hush little Mary, don't you cry." Tears came to our eyes and her mother's eyes. It was a God moment.

One day I was in Sunday school class when a man was attacked by an evil spirit and began to manifest. He could not help himself. His father was there trying to help, but to no avail. The Sunday school teacher was occupied with others who needed prayer. I got down on my knee and said, "By the power of the Holy Spirit, and by the name of Jesus Christ, spirit, I bind you up!"

Well, that caused the evil spirit to manifest even more! I said, "Lord Jesus, what does Tony need to know from you?"

Tony became still. I heard him say, "God loves me! I am good enough! He will honor me and heal me." I said, "Can he get up off the floor, Lord?" Tony said, "Yes I can." That was the beginning of Frank's and my relationship with Tony. We prayed for Tony's healing for years. And, those prayers were not in vain. Today, Tony is becoming a mighty warrior for the Lord. GOD'S WILL IS TO HEAL!

LESSONS LEARNED

Between people coming to me for healing and teaching the class, my time became very limited. People would regularly have to wait 3 to 4 weeks for an appointment for an inner healing. Once I had someone call and say, "If you don't see me, I'm going to go crazy!" I learned to refer those cases to the emergency room. It became my policy not to see people who would attempt such manipulative tactics.

Although I was not prepared for some things when I started this ministry, God took care of me. Now that I am more mature in this ministry, I see the importance of having certain things in place before getting involved in healing and deliverance ministry. If I were to give advice to someone interested in starting this type of healing ministry, this is what I would say:

1. Be sure you have been called to this type of ministry. This is nothing to take lightly and the enemy plays for high stakes.
2. If you are a lay-person, have a church covering.
3. Intercessory prayer is vitally important. You need to secure faithful people who will pray as you minister.
4. You should have some level of healing before you take anyone through the process.

CONCLUSION

God has forgiven us of all sins for which we have asked forgiveness. We; however, are often bound by things that happened in our past. Most issues we face stem from times of trauma when we felt unprotected. God is our protector. Jesus is all we need. Sometimes we just don't realize it.

We hope you read the rest of the book with an open heart and receive what God wants to reveal to you. The next section includes case studies of real people who have received healing through this healing process and our ministry. We hope you are able to learn from our mistakes and glean from our successes.

Finally, we would like to leave you with this final thought: "If God is for us who can be against us?" So Soar like Eagles!

God Bless You!

- Willie Frank and Sharon White

A PRACTICAL APPLICATION

CASE STUDY A: FEAR

One lady came to healing ministry because she was deathly afraid of flying. In the sessions, she would tremble even when we mentioned flying. All of her family would fly to different places for vacation and she would not go. At age 30, with three kids and a husband, she was miserable.

Sharon: Lord Jesus, take Tina back to a memory, a feeling, an emotion or picture and show her where she needs healing.

Tina: I remember when I was five years old. My mother and step-father took me and my sister to the drive-in. My mother would not let us see the picture. She made us lay down in the back seat of the car, but I remember hearing the worst sounds. People were on an airplane and I heard it crash. Everyone was yelling and screaming and no one came to help them.

By now, Tina was petrified. Her body had stiffened, her face had turned red and she was crying.

Sharon: Tina, Christ was right there. He was there with you. Lord Jesus, speak the truth to Tina.

Tina: God said, "I will never leave you. Nothing is too hard for me."

Sharon: Lord Jesus, is there anything else Tina needs to know?

Tina: God said, "The plane cannot do a thing I do not allow it to do. Put your trust in me. My angels have charge over you. I will not forsake you. It's o.k. I'll be there for you."

Sharon: Lord Jesus, is there anything else you need to say to Tina?

Tina: "You can fly if you choose to fly. I will be your security. Put your trust in me only."

Sharon: Tina, look around. Hear what God has said to you. On a scale of 0 to 10, where are you with this memory?

Tina: I feel fine. I am not afraid any longer. I have a sense of peace sitting in the back seat of the car.

Sharon: Are you sure?

Tina: Yes

Sharon: Thank you Jesus for the healing.

That day, Tina went through three other memories of fear. God healed her of each one. By the end of the session Tina no longer broke out in a cold sweat when discussing flying. Her homework assignment was to drive to the airport. Prior to the healing, she could not go to the airport without becoming immobilized with fear.

By the end of her second session, Tina had booked a 20 minute flight to Columbus, Ohio and made the trip without difficulty. This year, Tina's family is planning a trip to California (a four hour plane ride), and Tina is going! (Update: Tina is now an ordained minister and head of her deliverance ministry at her church. She flies on mission trips every two years. God is an awesome God. She is also trained in this healing process and has been equipping others for over 10 years.)

Thank you Lord for taking away a childhood fear that kept Tina in bondage for years.

CASE STUDY B: PORNOGRAPHY

Man 27: I had a major problem with pornography. I became hooked on porn at a very early age. I would take long lunch breaks and go to the local playboy store. Many times I would watch 3 to 4 pornographic videos a day. My wife was devastated. How could she compete with my habit? The truth of the matter is that she couldn't. I knew our marriage was in trouble, but I was hooked. A friend told me about the healing ministry. I said, "What the heck!" I had tried everything else including counseling, prayer, and the laying on of hands. I had even gone to an exorcist! Nothing worked! I really loved my movies.

When I first went for healing, God took me back to when I was a child: around age 5. My father left some magazines on the table and I was fascinated by them. Then I remembered standing under the church steps watching the women and girls walk up. I was a peeping Tom at age 7. At 10 my cousin came to live with us. She was 12 and for a while, we shared a room. She would dress in the bathroom but I would peep in on her through a hole in the door. By age 12 I was buying pornographic magazines when my friends were buying comic books. I would get an older man to buy the books for me and we would review them together. My entire life was centered on pornography. I also loved the Internet! There was so much stuff that was easily available and for free!

Each time I went for healing more and more was revealed to me. First, I realized that I had a generational sin in my life. My father had also been addicted to pornography. God took me back three generations and healed me from that. Next I was healed from the feeling of hopelessness. I felt hopeless! I felt that there was no way out. I felt that it would just happen over and over again. I had no options. This hopelessness came as a young boy at age 10. My father would continually blame me for things that I did not do. He would also physically punish me for crimes that I did not commit.

At the next session, God healed me from the lies that haunted me, "You are dirty, evil and perverted and that no one would ever love me". As a child, I remember I felt I was different from other kids in the family.

I was hooked on pornography and so ashamed of it. I did not think I could ever be free of this habit. It was a very long and hard battle, but today, I can finally say that the sin of pornography no longer has a hold on me. Today, I AM FREE! I thank God for the healing and my victory in Jesus Christ!

CASE STUDY C: ABANDONMENT

Connie was a 50-year-old woman that had been in and out of counseling all her life. When she came to me she was desperate.

Sharon:	Lord Jesus, take Connie to the memory, the feeling or the healing you want to give her tonight.
Connie:	I feel like a baby in my mother's womb. In fact, I am still in my mother's womb. I can feel the pressure and pull on my body. I'm choking on red fluid, it's blood.
	At this point, Connie turned red and was experiencing difficulty breathing.
Sharon:	Christ is right there with you. Lord Jesus, speak the truth to Connie.
	Connie's expression changed.
Connie:	Cleansed. I hear him saying, "You are cleansed; I have chosen you! I love you. I will be with you always."

Sharon: Connie, feel how it is not to be wounded and lonely. Lord Jesus, speak the truth to Connie.

Connie: I can see Him!

Sharon: What is He doing?

Connie: He's hugging me. He's cleaning off all the blood. He's saying, "I made you for a special purpose. I love you. My child, you are mine; you're going to be okay."

By now, Connie was in tears.

Sharon: Connie, is there anything bothering you in this memory?

Connie: No, it just feels so good to have God hold me.

Sharon: Thank you Jesus for the healing.

Connie had been an aborted baby but the abortion didn't work. All of her life she felt abandoned and unwanted. During other sessions she was completely healed of that lie. God will never abandon you.

CASE STUDY D: MOLESTATION

A man, age 35 came to see us for healing. He felt he had no control of his life.

Sharon:	Lord Jesus, speak the truth to Ted. Take him to the place where he needs healing.
Ted:	When I was growing up my father used to molest me and I felt badly because I enjoyed it.
Sharon:	Lord Jesus, speak the truth to Ted.
Ted:	He's saying, "You've done nothing wrong. I love you and I am with you."
Sharon:	Lord Jesus is there anything else you have to say to Ted?
Ted:	I felt like I couldn't get away from him (my dad).
Sharon:	Ted, do you feel like you were trapped with no way out?
Ted:	Yes.
Sharon:	Lord Jesus, Speak the truth to Ted.

Ted:	He's saying, "Fear not, I'm with you. I love you child; everything will be alright."
Ted:	But I got pleasure.
Sharon:	Lord Jesus, speak the truth to Ted about the pleasure he received from his father's molestation.
Ted:	He said, "It was not your fault. I forgave you a long time ago."
Sharon:	Ted, look around and see if you can feel Jesus' presence or see him.
Ted:	Jesus is there with his arms stretched out!
Sharon:	Do you want to go to him?
Ted:	Yes, He's holding me!

Ted began to smile. I knew God had done a work on Ted that day. You see. God released him of his shame and guilt. Ted no longer felt out of control. His whole life changed.

CASE STUDY E: DIVORCE

Woman Age 40: I was married for 10 years to a man that I truly loved. The first seven years were like a storybook. We had purchased a house and were planning on children. Around this time, my husband found out that he couldn't have children. At first, it was hard for both of us to accept; much more for him than for me.

Soon my husband started acting differently. I attributed it to his not accepting the fact that he could not have children. He began to miss appointments and not show up for work. One Thanksgiving, he lowered the bomb on me. He no longer wanted to live with me. He felt he needed a break. He moved out and told me he would be staying with his father. I was devastated! I was facing my worse fear. What had I done to cause this?

Well, for over a year Calvin, my husband, came by to see me on Sundays or whenever. I would call his father's home during the week rarely catching him at home. I felt like I was going out of my mind. I loved my husband and I needed him to come home. I didn't care what it took. I needed Calvin to come home.

A friend told me about Frank and Sharon's healing ministry. I was desperate! I wanted to know why. What was it about me that made my husband leave? In the first session, Jesus healed me of the need for NEED! Yes, I was the child of an alcoholic and although I wasn't aware of it, I had all the classic co-dependencies that children of alcoholics have. I was in the same vicious cycle my mother had been in with my father.

In the second session, God healed me of the feeling of powerlessness. He told me, "I will be there to comfort you. I will give you peace. I will deal with your husband's sin; there is nothing you can do to stop him."

Then I saw Jesus and He lifted me up and held me. What a sense of peace and joy! He said, "You will have to be strong and make choices that Calvin cannot make. It is not your fault. This was not the result of anything you did or didn't do."

After that, I asked my husband to come home and to go to counseling. Calvin thought I was joking. He had begun to enjoy the freedom of being married without the responsibility. He still paid all the bills. God revealed to me that there was a woman in his life.

By the third session, God had healed me of so many childhood memories that I was able to make many important steps. I stopped calling Calvin's father every day. I changed the locks on the house. I told Calvin that he had to make the choice to come home or to leave.

Calvin chose to leave.

For every action there is a reaction. Did I still love my husband? Yes. I had to set some boundaries.

Calvin filed for divorce. I was devastated again! I asked God to reveal what was happening in Calvin's life. The next day, I saw Calvin with his girlfriend and her family at a restaurant.

At the fourth session, God helped me to face reality and I signed the divorce papers.

After that, everything changed! Calvin began to call me every day wanting to come see me. I knew that he and I still needed counseling. Calvin refused counseling and I know that God is still dealing with him. I continue to pray for my husband and believe that God can bring us back together. I thank God for my healing. (Update: Calvin chose not to go to healing. We have been divorced for five years. God has brought a wonderful God-fearing man into my life.

CASE STUDY F: ANGER

Martin was a new convert at our church. He was originally from Mexico and seemed angry all the time. Martin loved the Lord but he could not control his temper. Frank asked Martin to come to a session and he did. After we prayed, God took Martin to a memory at age 4.

Martin: I see my mother and she's beating me because I would not cut the TV off.

Sharon: How do you feel?

Martin: I am angry and it's hopeless. Nothing I do will please her.

Sharon: So you're saying, "You're angry and hopeless?"

Martin: Yes.

Sharon: Lord Jesus, speak the truth to Martin.

Martin: Jesus is right there with me. He's saying that I must forgive my mother. He said he loved me and that I have to love. He told me to look at how the prophets were persecuted. Then He told me to walk in the light.

By now, Martin was crying. God continued to speak. Martin began speaking in Spanish. Jesus healed that memory and Martin kept coming back for more healing. One memory at a time, Martin was healed of fear, anger, abandonment and hopelessness. The unique thing about Martin was that Jesus always healed him in his native tongue. Sometimes Martin would even translate for us. God heals us in His own way.